Essential Question
What actions can we take to get along with others?

Winning Friends

by Max Olsen   illustrated by Sole Otero

Chapter 1
Ignored..2

Chapter 2
A Plan..6

Chapter 3
I'll Do It.....................................10

Chapter 4
The Contest.................................13

Respond to Reading..........................16

PAIRED READ Empathy: The Answer to Bullying..17

Focus on Literary Elements..................20

Chapter 1
Ignored

"I made it!" said Jalissa, running out of the drama teacher's office. "I'm in the school musical!"

"I knew you could do it!" said Ella.

Ella and Jalissa had met in kindergarten. Since then, they did almost everything together—from summer camp to learning the violin.

Ella had wanted be in the musical, too, but she had been sick when the **auditions** were held. So Jalissa had tried out without Ella, and now Jalissa was in the play without her.

As usual, the girls sat together at lunch the next day. But Jalissa talked to Maddy and Jakeira, who were also in the musical, and Ella felt left out.

Maddy asked, "Have you learned your lines yet, Jalissa?"

"No," Jalissa replied. "Let's practice together before the next musical **rehearsal**!"

Ella wished she could join in their conversation, but she was not in the play.

After school, Ella invited Jalissa to shoot some baskets.

"Sorry, but I'm reading lines with Maddy and Jakeira," said Jalissa before she hurried off.

It was as if Jalissa didn't want to hang out with her anymore. "I hope this doesn't last much longer," thought Ella.

But the next day was the same, and so was the day after that. All Jalissa talked about was how much fun the musical was. Ella felt like Jalissa was **taunting** her, and that she wanted Ella to feel left out.

Ella needed to do something. When school got out on Friday, Ella raced after Jalissa. She was in such a hurry that she didn't watch where she was going and almost **collided** with her teacher. "Jalissa!" she called, "do you want to come to the lake with my family on Saturday?"

"Sorry, Ella," said Jalissa. "I'm going to a slumber party at Jakeira's."

Ella asked hesitantly, "Don't you want to hang out with me anymore, Jalissa?"

Jalissa sighed. "I'm just busy with the play. Why don't you come and watch the next rehearsal on Monday?"

Ella agreed. Maybe if she got to know Jalissa's new friends, she wouldn't feel left out.

> **STOP AND CHECK**
>
> Why does Ella invite Jalissa to the lake with her family?

Chapter 2
A Plan

Ella missed Jalissa at the lake that weekend. Ella hoped that going to the rehearsal on Monday would improve things, but she was wrong.

When she walked to the auditorium with Jalissa and her friends from the play, they all talked about the slumber party. Ella felt bad because she hadn't been invited.

In the auditorium, Ella sat in the front row while the others got up on the stage. Once again, there was Jalissa, having fun without her.

When the director **dismissed** the cast for the afternoon, Jalissa jumped down from the stage and left with Maddy, Jakeira, and another girl.

Ella caught up with them and asked, "What are you guys up to now?"

"We have to practice our dance routine," replied Jalissa.

"Cool," said Ella. "I can be your audience."

"But it will be really boring for you," said Jalissa. "Sorry, Ella. I'll catch you tomorrow."

Ella was close to tears. She had sat through two hours of a boring rehearsal, hoping to spend some time with Jalissa, and now Jalissa was telling her to go away.

It was so unfair. She didn't want to be too **protective** of their friendship, but she had to find a way to remind Jalissa that they were best friends.

On the way home, Mom stopped at the library to return some books. When she came back, she handed Ella a leaflet.

"Look at this," she said.

The leaflet was about a talent contest, and first prize was a trip to a theme park in Florida. It was as if a light switched on in Ella's head.

"Jalissa and I should enter," she exclaimed. "If we play a violin duet, we might win!"

And playing the violin together would remind Jalissa that they were best friends.

That night, Ella called Jalissa. "Hey, Jalissa, I have a cool idea!"

"Oh, yeah?" Jalissa did not sound interested, and Ella realized this might be harder than she had thought.

"There's a talent contest in two weeks," Ella continued. "The prize is a trip to WonderWorld in Florida! We should play a violin duet."

"I don't know," said Jalissa. "I'm really busy."

"Come on," said Ella, wishing she had an **ally** to help her convince Jalissa. "We can practice when you don't have rehearsals."

"A trip to WonderWorld would be cool," said Jalissa, "but I don't want anything to get in the way of the musical."

"Please? We can play a piece we already know."

"I need to think about it. I'll call you back," replied Jalissa.

Ella stared at the phone after she hung up. How would she and Jalissa stay friends if this idea didn't work?

STOP AND CHECK

Why did Jalissa want to call Ella back about the talent show?

Chapter 3
I'll Do It

Ten minutes later, Ella's phone rang. It was Jalissa.

"I'll do it," she said.

"Really?" said Ella. Jalissa did not sound enthusiastic, but she had agreed.

"I don't know if it's a good idea, because the musical is a lot of work, but Mom says we should do it."

Ella felt like telling her to forget it, but maybe Jalissa's attitude, or mood, would change once they got started.

"We could have our first practice tomorrow during lunch," Ella suggested. "Meet you in the music room?"

"Okay, you bring the music," said Jalissa **half-heartedly**. She seemed bored.

"And *you* bring a better mood," thought Ella.

The next day, the girls met at lunch. "Bach's Double Concerto in D Minor is boring," said Jalissa as she unpacked her violin.

"But it's our best piece," replied Ella.

Jalissa tuned her violin. "I don't see how it'll help us win the contest."

Ella thought Jalissa was trying to upset her on purpose, but all she said was, "From the top?"

They began playing, and for the first time in ages, it felt like they were friends again. The music was **intervening**, making Ella forget the **conflict** between them.

"That was pretty good," said Ella when they'd finished.

Jalissa shrugged, and the warmth Ella had felt was suddenly gone.

"Let's go over that hard passage again," Ella suggested.

"Okay, but then I have to go," said Jalissa.

Ella sighed. She could tell that this was going to be a long **struggle**—a fight all the way to the end.

The girls played the passage again, but it still wasn't right. "One more time," Ella said.

"I have to go!" snapped Jalissa **abruptly**. "There's a cast meeting in five minutes."

It was too much for Ella. She had to say something.

"Jalissa, you're not being fair. You agreed to enter the talent contest, and I didn't do anything wrong."

"Maybe I shouldn't have," replied Jalissa, slamming her violin case shut. "I quit," she said, and then stormed out.

STOP AND CHECK

Why did Jalissa quit the talent show contest?

Chapter 4
The Contest

That night, Ella had never felt so miserable in her life. She had failed to save her friendship with Jalissa. Ella was just about to flop down on her bed and cry when the phone rang. It was Jalissa.

"Ella?" said Jalissa. "I've been thinking about what you said. Playing the violin with you today made me remember how we used to hang out together. I guess I haven't been a good friend and ... I'm really sorry."

Ella did not know what to say.

"I was so excited to be in the musical," Jalissa continued, "it's all I've been thinking about. Do you think you can forgive me?"

Ella didn't hesitate to reply, "Of course! You're my best friend."

Just then, Ella heard Jalissa's violin. "Want to play the duet?" asked Jalissa.

"Over the phone?" laughed Ella.

"Why not?" said Jalissa, laughing, too.

From then on, the two friends practiced often. It wasn't easy with musical rehearsals, but they did it. When the day of the talent contest arrived, the friends felt **confident**.

They were the last act to perform. When they heard the **announcement** over the microphone: "And now, Ella Chavez and Jalissa Browne," the girls walked across the stage, stopped in the center, then lifted their violins together.

When they finished, the clapping went on and on. "They liked us," whispered Ella.

"Maybe they're just clapping because it's over," Jalissa answered nervously.

The clapping stopped as the announcer walked onto the stage.

"The judges have had a difficult time choosing the winner," he began. "Third prize, a gift certificate for ten music downloads, goes to … Maurice and Jerome Leigh for their hip-hop dance!" Ella and Jalissa clapped **politely** for the dance team.

"Second prize, four double movie passes, goes to … Ella Chavez and Jalissa Browne, for their beautiful violin duet!"

The audience was clapping, but Ella was not sure how she felt. Second place was good, but they didn't win. She turned to Jalissa, who was already on her way to the stage.

"Come on!" Jalissa grinned.

As the girls walked through the parking lot with their parents afterward, Jalissa said, "I don't care about not winning first prize. We may not have won the contest, but we did win back our friendship."

> **STOP AND CHECK**
>
> What helped the girls become friends again?

Summarize

Use key details from *Winning Friends* to summarize the story. Your graphic organizer may help.

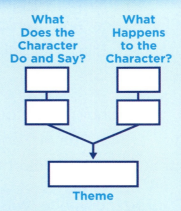

Text Evidence

1. What does Ella do to try to save her friendship with Jalissa? **THEME**

2. Find the word *attitude* on page 10. What clues help you figure out the meaning? **VOCABULARY**

3. Write about why the author wrote about Jalissa and Ella and the talent contest. What message can you learn from this story? **WRITE ABOUT READING**

Genre | **Expository Text**

Compare Texts
Read about a program some schools use to help students understand and respect each other's feelings.

EMPATHY
The Answer to Bullying

What is bullying? Bullying is when one person does things to hurt another person over and over in some way. A bully might hit people, or they might hurt people's feelings by calling them names or by making threats.

Why do bullies hurt others? One reason is that they want to control other people. Another reason is that they feel bad about themselves. Bullies do not feel empathy for the people they bully. *Empathy* means to be able to imagine how another person feels.

Roots of Empathy is a program used in some schools. The program teaches students skills to get along with others, and it works to reduce mean behavior, such as bullying. It also teaches kind behavior, such as sharing and helping. The program focuses on empathy.

Mary Gordon started Roots of Empathy. The program began in Canada in 1996. It has grown since then. Now schools in many other countries use it, including schools in the United States, England, and New Zealand.

Mary Gordon talks to people about bullying.

The Roots of Empathy program asks a parent to visit a classroom with his or her baby. Students observe the baby. Then an instructor encourages students to talk about what they saw. The parent and baby return every three weeks of the school year, so students get to watch the baby grow and learn.

Students participate in the Roots of Empathy program.

Mary Gordon believes that studying a baby's emotions helps students. The students understand their own feelings better. They also learn to understand other people's feelings.

Studies show that the Roots of Empathy program works. Students who participate are less likely to become bullies. And people who have empathy are less likely to hurt other people.

Make Connections

How can spending time with a parent and baby help people get along together? ESSENTIAL QUESTION

How could Jalissa have acted differently if she had thought about Ella's feelings? TEXT TO TEXT

Focus on Literary Elements

Mood Writers use words to create a mood or feeling in a story. Writers can use words to create a mood that is cheerful, sad, anxious, or scary.

Read and Find Look at the way the writer describes Ella and Jalissa on page 12. The words *snapped* and *abruptly* create a tense mood. Now look at the way the writer describes Ella and Jalissa on page 15. The words *grinned* and *friendship* create a happy mood.

Your Turn

What kind of mood do these sentences make you think of? Tell which words show the mood. How do they make you feel?

The crash of thunder shook the room awake.

"You just don't understand!" Stevie growled. Then she stormed out of the room, slamming the door behind her with a boom.

Mark's eyes twinkled at the thought. Slowly, a wide grin spread across his face.